Chimera

A play

D0088594

Alec Baron

Samuel French – London
New York – Sydney – Toronto – Hollywood

CHARACTERS

Kate, a paraplegic of twenty-nine
Emma, her friend, the same age
Mrs Ponsello, her "treasure"
Panda

Other plays by Alec Baron
published by Samuel French

The Big Cats
Company Come
Dress Rehearsal

CHIMERA

The living-room cum bedroom of a country cottage.   An early evening in winter

There are two doors, one leading to the front door and the other, upstage, to the kitchen. The bed has a swinging pole, chain and handle (a polly-perch), of the type used by a disabled person. Sitting up in the bed is a large, soft toy, a panda. There is an easel with a canvas on it, its back to the audience, and a few other canvases lean against the wall here and there. Over by the window is a small table on which there are books, newspapers and painting items

When the CURTAIN *rises, the lamps are lit and the curtains drawn, although it is still early on a winter's evening. Mrs Ponsello, a clean-looking country woman of about fifty, is turning down the bed. The telephone rings. She looks up, expecting someone else to answer it, and carries on working*

Kate (*off, calling*) Would you answer that, Mrs Ponsello, please?
Mrs Ponsello Yes, dear. (*Into the phone*) Hello. ... Yes, it is. ... Not at the moment you can't. ... Where is she? She's in the lav. ... (*Shouting*) The *loo*... the *toilet*. ... I don't know, she's slow at these things.

There is the sound of a plane going over

Hang on a tick, I didn't get that, there's a plane going over. ... How do you get here? Y' just drive into the village and ask for

Hawthorne Cottage. ... Well where are you? ... Y' don't know! Now I can't tell you which way to come if I don't know where y' are, can I? ... All right, I'll tell 'er. (*She replaces the receiver and returns to the bed. She lays out Kate's nightclothes and a dressing-gown and tucks the panda in on one side*) There y' are, Panda, 'ow's that? Comfy? (*She crosses to the small table and straightens the books etc.*)

Kate enters in a wheelchair, sitting on a thick cushion. She is a very pretty girl of twenty-nine, paralysed from the waist down. There is no hint of self-pity when she speaks; she seems a very happy person

Kate Who was that?

Mrs Ponsello Nobody, I was talking to Panda.

Kate On the telephone.

Mrs Ponsello Oh -- some woman.

Kate (*after a pause, pleasantly*) Well, what did she want?

Mrs Ponsello She's coming to see you — wanted to know how to find the place. So I told her.

Kate Did she give her name?

Mrs Ponsello Yes, but there was a plane going over. Something like Mrs Evelyn. I've turned your bed down.

Kate Thanks. Off you go then. (*She wheels herself towards the bed*)

Mrs Ponsello Yes. (*She is hesitant. She gets her coat but doesn't put it on*) There's — there's summat I've to tell you, but I 'aven't bin able to get it out. I, er ... I did tell you me 'usband lost his job, didn't I? Well 'e's found another.

Kate Oh I am pleased. Where?

Mrs Ponsello That's just it. 'E wants to go back.

Kate To Italy?

Mrs Ponsello Cousin of 'is has sort of little supermarket — in Milan. Offered 'im a job.

Kate Why, that's splendid!

Mrs Ponsello Yeh ... except I ... I'll 'ave to be goin' with 'im.

Kate smiles, quickly dispelling a slight shadow over her face

Kate Of course. Of course you will.

Mrs Ponsello I didn't want to go. I didn't want *him* to go.

Kate Oh, but you have to.

Mrs Ponsello I was thinkin' of *you*. What'll ...?

Kate I'll be sorry to see you go, Mrs Ponsello, of course, but you must stay with your husband. I can't say I won't miss you ...

Mrs Ponsello I'll miss you too. It'll be four years Monday after Easter I've bin comin' to you. We worked it out last night, Nino and me.

Kate Is it really four years? (*Forcibly changing the subject after a quick pause; cheerfully*) I thought of baking a cake tomorrow but if you won't be here ... I'd have to eat it all myself and that would be very silly of me.

Mrs Ponsello I've tried makin' enquiries in't village. I was hopin' to find someone to take over like, but I've not bin able to come up wi' anybody.

Kate So the whole village knows ...?

Mrs Ponsello What, that Nino and me are goin'? Well, we've bin gettin' rid of the furniture. They 'ad to know.

Kate (*smiling*) Selling up? Going for good then? When?

Mrs Ponsello Two weeks' time. Only I couldn't bring meself to tell you until now. Nino bought Mester Duckworth's old van yesterday. It's pretty old but it's in perfect workin' order. We're goin' by road. So I'm givin' you two weeks' notice.

Kate That's very considerate of you, Mrs Ponsello, we only arranged one week either way, if you remember.

Mrs Ponsello (*hesitantly*) Y' wouldn't think of goin' back to what's-its-name, would you? That 'ospital? I think that'd be best for you. I mean in case y' didn't find anybody to —

Kate If I don't find anybody, Mrs Ponsello, I shall manage on my own. I'm only paralysed from the waist down, the rest of me is like Mr Duckworth's van, in perfect working order.

Mrs Ponsello *You* can't clean this house – especially after the mess it gets in when you've bin paintin' ...

Kate I'll just have to not dirty it then, won't I?

Mrs Ponsello What about the shoppin'?

Kate I've got the telephone.

Mrs Ponsello They won't *all* deliver. Not round 'ere they won't.

Kate Please don't worry about me, Mrs Ponsello. I'll cope. Be off now, you must have lots to do. And I'm ready for bed.

Mrs Ponsello Y' know, I think you're bloody marvellous, the way you manage. And always so cheerful with it. Some of 'em in this village want for nothin' and do nothin' but moan. Real tonic, you are. (*She moves to the door, then turns*) I'll call round in't mornin' — I'm doin' Mrs Coombs tomorrow for 't last time, so it's not out o' me way — just to see if y' want summat fetchin'.

Kate Thank you. That's very kind of you.

Mrs Ponsello Good-night then. I'll drop the latch.

Kate Yes. Thanks. Good-night.

Mrs Ponsello goes

There is the sound of a plane going over. Kate wheels herself across the room as if to do something then stops, forgetting what she intended to do. The worry is visible behind her fixed, forced smile

(*Hating having to be grateful for everything*) Thank *you*, Mrs Ponsello. That's very *kind* of you, Mrs Ponsello. *Thank* you! I *do* appreciate it! Thanks *very* much! (*She pulls herself together with an effort*) What do you think of that, Panda? We're losing our treasure! Some bleeding bombshell, eh? I just couldn't start breaking anyone else into our silly ways! (*Short pause*) Italy! That's where we always wanted to go, wasn't it, Panda? Maybe we will yet, one day.

Panda Get on! *You'll* never make it!

When Panda speaks, the mouth moves and the animal almost comes alive. Kate is quite accustomed to being addressed by Panda

Kate You never know. We could fly. They say folk like you and me who are a bit helpless get well looked after in planes.

Panda Forget it! *You* can't make it to the next village, never mind Italy!

Kate I think that's the advantage of marrying an Italian. You do get to see Italy once in a while.

Panda OK, so that's the advantage. We won't mention the drawbacks.

Kate You're a cynic, that's your trouble. (*She moves behind Panda and cuddles him*) You'd like to go to Italy, wouldn't you? Come on, admit it. Just think, we could paint all day, outside. They say the light there is marvellous.

Panda Why don't you give in! *You can't paint!* Why do you keep fooling yourself? Those things of yours are just daubs!

Kate Everyone says they're excellent.

Panda They're just being kind and you know it. Anyway, what's the point, we're boxed in here. It's a bloody cage, this place!

Kate (*suddenly irritated; shouting*) All right! Do you mind if I at least rattle the bars! (*She moves and calms down*) Siena, Verona! Padua! Just imagine! Maybe *we'll* meet an Italian, you never know. And *you'd* be all right, there's spaghetti and cannelloni. Tastes a bit like bamboo sometimes.

Panda I'm not having no Italian in this bed, thanks very much.

Kate If I find one you'll have him and you'll like him. Do you hear? (*She moves to the bed*) I think I'll come to bed, Panda, eh? What do you say?

Panda Oh come on, it's early yet.

Kate What is there to stay up for?

Panda Switch on the telly.

Kate I'm tired of telly. Same damn thing every night. Besides we slept badly last night, both of us. I know I did, and I kept waking you up, didn't I? Sorry about that. (*During the following, she starts to get undressed, struggling out of her clothes and into her nightclothes*)

Panda We're going to be in real trouble, you and me, aren't we, when Mrs P goes?

Kate We'll manage. You'll have to help me.

Panda Me? I'm more helpless than you are!

Kate I am not helpless.

Panda Don't make me laugh. You've no legs!

Kate I get about, don't I? I've got arms. I cope with the old bowel and bladder problems, don't I?

Panda Only just! You can't even reach the cupboard over the sink.

Kate I'm going to have that cupboard lowered.

Panda Do you know how long you've been saying that? You'll never get it done, you're just fooling yourself like with everything else.

Kate I'll have to now, won't I?

Panda I've heard that before too.

Kate You're in a cruel mood tonight, aren't you? Just when I need a bit of kindness from someone.

Panda Then let's change the subject before I really say something you won't like.

Kate Yes, let's! (*Pause*) I wonder who it was, on the phone.

Panda Another of those damned social workers for sure, coming to mess us about. I wish they'd leave us alone.

Kate I don't know how you can say that!

Panda I can't stand those do-gooders!

Kate You're horrid, do you know that? If it weren't for them we'd hardly see anyone.

Panda And whose fault is that?

Kate Oh please, Panda, don't start again!

Panda Moving to this dead-alive hole! Not letting anyone know our address! Not even Emma!

Kate Panda, I've asked you – please forget about Emma.

Panda (*amazed*) Forget about Emma? Your best friend!

Kate All right. So what!

Panda Not only your best friend, your only friend.

Kate That's not true.

Panda She was my friend too, remember. Very fond of me, Emma was.

Kate She didn't want me hanging round her neck like a dead weight.

Panda Stubborn, that's what you are. Bloody obstinate! The least you could have done was write and tell her where we are. You can still.

Kate What's the point? She lives six thousand miles away. She's married.

Panda Lucky bugger! (*Seeking agreement*) Eh?

Kate What was there to write about? I kept writing the same letter every time. Nothing worth writing about ever happens to us.

Panda Something happened today, didn't it? Mrs P happened today! I've just thought of a title for our autobiography — *Alone and Paralysed*. It'll be a bestseller.

Kate (*ignoring this*) You and I have to be content watching what other people get up to. We can look into that tube and watch. And that's it.

Panda Here it comes. The old self-pity again. Wallowing in it as usual.

Kate That's not true. I do not wallow in self-pity!

Panda You do with me.

Kate You're different. (*Pause. She is now in her nightclothes*) It's not the end of the world. We'll survive. Only I'll be expecting a lot more from you, you'll have to damn well pull your weight. (*She heaves herself into bed, using the polly-perch*) That's all I ever seem to do, pull my weight about, and I'm not getting any lighter, either. Have you seen these muscles? We'll have to cut down on our bamboo, won't we?

Panda Huh!

Kate Right. Are you ready for bye-byes?

Panda Bye-byes! For Christ's sake grow up! What's the matter with saying sleep? Bye-byes! Really!

Kate (*pulling the blanket over his shoulders tenderly*) That's enough now. Night-night, grumpy. (*She turns out the light*)

Panda Bye-byes!

In the dim light remaining we see her put her arm around Panda and snuggle in. There is the sound of a plane passing over. After some time there is a ring at the bell. Kate doesn't move at first, but when the bell rings a second time she jumps up and turns on the lights

Kate There's someone at the door!

Panda Mrs P's forgotten her knick-knacks again, silly twit!

Kate Mrs P's got a key. (*She swings her legs out of bed with an effort, pulls on her dressing-gown and heaves herself into the wheelchair*)

She goes out to answer the door

(*Off*) Who is it?

Emma (*off, excitedly*) Is that Kate? It's me – Emma.

Panda Don't get excited, it can't be *our* Emma.

Kate (*off*) Emma! Just a minute, the latch is a bit high.

Panda You were going to get that latch altered, weren't you?

Kate (*off, struggling*) There!

The door is heard opening

(*Off*) Emma! Emma!

Emma (*off*) Kate! Darling! Darling Kate!

Emma comes in, wheeling Kate – they are both in tears. Emma is the same age as Kate, not as good looking but smartly dressed

Dear, darling Kate! Were you in bed? Oh, I am sorry.

Kate No, I was just about to —

Emma But it's early.

Kate I thought I'd have a specially early night.

Emma I rang to say I was on my way.

Kate (*smiling through tears*) It was you then – that rang. Do you know, I had a strange feeling ... I don't know why ... I didn't dare ...

Emma Come on now, tell me, why did you stop writing? Why didn't you let me know where you had moved to?

Kate How did you find me?

Emma Wait, let me get my coat off. (*She throws her coat over a chair*) Why the hell did you cut me off like that? You *must* have got my letters because they didn't come back.

Kate Yes, I got them. Well, I got some.

Emma Why didn't you reply?

Kate There was nothing to write about. It's a very quiet place this. Each day for me is just like the day before. All kinds of exciting things were happening to you, living in Los Angeles. Hollywood - - all that glamour! Going on holiday to exotic places, and to shows and concerts — and everything! You had so much to write about. You didn't want to get the same old dull letter from me every time.

Emma Dull? It was exciting for me just to see an English postage stamp, just to see your handwriting on the envelope. I was longing to know about *you*. Everything! Whether you were getting any better, what the doctors said ...

Kate But I told you ...

Emma Well, what you were reading, what you were doing, who you were seeing. And your folks – I mean your mother – how's she?

Kate Didn't I tell you? She died.

Emma Oh I am sorry. Who lives here with you then?

Kate Just Panda.

Emma (*delighted, as if referring to an old friend*) Oh, you've still got Panda! (*Seeing him*) Hello, Panda. (*Going over and hugging him*) I haven't seen you since Paris!

Kate Panda loved Paris, didn't you, Panda?

Emma And how long have you and Panda been living alone then?

Kate A long time now. Four years in fact. Mother died not long after we moved in here. She never really recovered from the accident.

Emma (*unable to put it off any longer*) Kate – I can't tell you how devastated I was when you wrote me about the accident. (*Looking at her legs*) Is there nothing they can do?

Kate It's not all that bad. If you've no bread, you eat cake. I've swapped my legs for wheels, that's all. If you can't walk, then you ride.

Emma How did it happen? You never said in your letter you know.

Kate There was nothing to tell, it was just an ordinary accident, they happen all the time.

Emma That's what you said, but I'd – I'd like to know. Was it horrible?

Kate It was all over in seconds. Father was driving. There was a car coming towards us — its front tyre burst and it hit us, almost head-on. Father died as I told you, so did the other driver. I was in the back, behind Father. We were trapped for over an hour. An eternity! Mother was in front next to Father – she managed to scramble out. I think it was worst of all for her, she was hysterical and unable to do anything to help us. I felt so sorry for her.

Emma Your father was killed instantly then?

Kate I wish he had been. No, he died just before they got us out, about five minutes before. I was able to hold his hand, and talk to him, the whole time. It was, like you say, horrible. Blood all over the place. I don't like to think about it!

Emma My poor Kate!

Kate Mother took it very badly. It left a chronic abscess on her memory. She couldn't sleep – and when she did drop off she had terrible nightmares, woke up screaming. She never really recovered, although they said she had.

Emma Who said?

Kate The insurance people. But they didn't quibble about Daddy and me. Well, they couldn't, could they? Eventually the other fellow's insurance paid out.

Emma I can't tell you what it does to me, seeing you like this, in a wheelchair. I'm sorry, Kate, I have to say it. You were so ...

Kate I'm lucky really, I was covered by insurance, so I'm at least independent. I've met people who were born like this – and poor. They're the ones to be sorry for.

Emma The shock must have been – awful ...

Kate Your mind doesn't take it in at first, doesn't accept it. You keep thinking you're going to wake up one morning and find you can move your legs as you've always done, and it was all a dream – that's your mind being kind to your body.

Emma Isn't there *something* they can do?

Kate Not with a spinal-cord injury, apparently. It's non-progressive, thank the Lord.

Emma What does that mean?

Kate It means I shouldn't get any worse than I am now. Their only comfort was that it's better to be paralysed from the waist down rather than up. I became very aggressive at first, towards everybody, although they said this was a normal reaction. In fact the whole pantomime becomes more sort of natural, or normal, as time progresses. But we're talking about me. I want to know about you. When did you come? Are you back for good?

Emma I've been here three weeks, and I fly back tomorrow, to LA. This is my last night here, and I've only just found you.

Kate Tomorrow!

Emma What a time I had finding you! Do you know the people at your old house have no idea where you are?

Kate We didn't tell them.

Emma For heaven's sake, why not?

Kate Mother and I decided to go — you know — ex-directory. Mother was tired of everybody sympathizing.

Panda Liar! Mother was against it! *You* decided!

Emma does not hear this

Emma I rang the university — they gave me your old address where I'd already been. So did everybody else. It was just as if you'd disappeared into thin air. Then this afternoon I suddenly got the idea you might have been at Stoke Mandeville, so I rang there. In desperation really. I said I was a near relative over from America and they gave me this address and phone number. I came straightaway. I mean, you are one of the main reasons I made this trip.

Kate uses her arms to lift herself clear of the chair

  What are you doing?

Kate Don't mind me — I have to do this pretty regularly to get some air to my bottom, or I get pressure sores. Try and ignore it. Tell me, how are your folks?

Emma No different. My other reason for this trip is that I thought I ought to pay them a visit before the baby is born. It won't be so easy afterwards.

Kate You're pregnant! Emma darling ...! That's terrific!

Emma Well I'm only just pregnant. Doesn't show yet, does it?

Kate Is this the first? I hardly dare ask.

Emma No, I've another three back home.

Kate (*almost believing her*) Really?

Emma Or is it six? I don't remember. No, this is me making my début.

Kate And how's Larry? I'll bet he's delighted.

Emma Fathers just take these things for granted, didn't you know? They don't get all excited, handing round cigars to everybody like

they do in the movies. It's part of that old masculine sang-froid. You
remember what sang-froid is?

Kate Of course I do — a bloody cold. Will I ever forget!

They both laugh at the memory

That was the best holiday I ever had.

Emma Mine too. (*Laughing*) Remember that night on rue Picot?

Kate (*laughing*) Do you know, I've never figured out, even now,
what made them think we were prostitutes. Weren't we green!

Emma It was that miniskirt of yours.

Kate Everybody was wearing miniskirts that year.

Emma You had more wiggle.

Kate Fancy straying on to the pro's regular beat by accident! How
were we to know?

Emma I don't know about sang-froid, there was nothing cold about
those guys. Can I let you into a secret? Larry's never approached that
standard ever since we got married.

Kate (*without self-pity*) I didn't know it at the time but those few
days were the culmination of my love-life too. The high spot — and
the final fling. I'm so glad we let our hair down.

Emma I think we let everything down.

Kate Especially our parents and teachers.

Emma I didn't mean that.

They giggle like schoolgirls

Kate I know you didn't.

Emma We shouldn't have taken their money though.

Kate Why not?

Emma Not every night!

Kate We were running short, don't you remember?

Emma That was your fault, you were supposed to work out how
much we would need. You were miles out.

Kate I expected to get treated. We always had been before. But we
were paying for ourselves, everywhere.

Emma The only thing I really regret is taking that money. Sort of cheapens the ——

Kate I've thought about that. I have a theory that when a man pays for his pleasure he's more fun because he's less inhibited.

Emma I'll take your word for that. You'd had a lot more experience of men than I had.

Kate Oh come on.

Emma Of course you had. Fellers were buzzing around you like wasps around a picnic, all the time. In swarms. Even at school, *before* university. Hey, do you remember that time you were nearly expelled?

Kate (*relishing the thought*) Yes, over Simon Wicklow from Gretton High. The rugby captain.

Emma He *was* expelled, poor lad. And Gretton lost every match after that.

Kate Didn't do *him* any harm. He's managing director of a chain of furniture stores, I often see his picture in the paper. Drives a Rolls with a personalized number plate. SJW1. If he hadn't been expelled he'd have been a dentist.

Emma Expect they're all married by now, surrounded with kids.

Kate (*a shadow*) Yes. (*Quickly clearing*) But look — let me offer you something. How about some tea?

Emma I couldn't really. I had a huge meal before I came.

Kate A drink! Tell you what — there's a bottle of gin I won in a local raffle last summer. Never been opened. I'll get it. (*She starts to move*)

Emma Where is it? In the back? (*She wheels Kate towards the scullery*)

Kate I don't think we've ever had a drink in this house. Mother was absolutely against alcohol.

They exit

(*Off*) That's it, up there on the shelf. The glasses are in this cupboard. I'll hold that.

Emma wheels Kate back in. Kate has two glasses and a bottle of gin which she is trying to open

Emma Here, let me —
Kate No, I want to open it.

Emma takes the glasses and puts them on the small table as Kate opens the bottle and pours

I've no tonic water. Would you like ordinary water with it?
Emma Let's be devils and drink it neat.
Kate (*raising her glass; a toast*) Emma, this is the most wonderful day I've had in years. Here's to it!
Emma Here's to it.

They drink

Bottoms up, as the homos say in San Francisco.

They drain the glasses and laugh unrestrainedly

Kate Pass your glass, I'll fill it up. (*She fills both glasses*) A votre santé.

They drink

And what's it like in good old California? You've developed an American accent, you know.
Emma Had to, on account of my job, but I've been trying to drop it whilst I'm here.
Kate Oh, you work?
Emma I did do. Given it up now. Just sat by a telephone. When it rang I sprang into action. I got tired of guys saying "What's that?" "What's that you're saying?" They don't hoot with delight at an English accent like they did in wartime, you know.
Kate You hardly needed a degree in English for that!
Emma You haven't made much use of your qualifications either, for that matter.
Kate All that work we did!
Emma What a waste!

Kate Come on, empty that glass.

They drink

How did you get on with Larry's parents? I remember how scared
you were they wouldn't like you.

Emma They're OK, I guess. We don't see much of them. They
moved out to Fresno a while back. We rent their house, you know.
Well, it's convenient for Larry's work.

Kate Still doing photography?

Emma Oh he gave that up a while back. Didn't I write you about
that? He's a newsreel cameraman for a TV company. You probably
see a lot of his stuff, it's always going out on satellite. He covers
things like — oh, presidential elections, riots, Oscar ceremonies,
things like that.

Kate Oscar ceremonies? I watched that. Just think ...!

Emma Has his own crew now, and transport, fully equipped for
live transmission. They send him all over the place.

Kate Must be doing well then.

Emma What about you? What do you live on?

Kate Oh I'm OK. We bought this house with the compensation
money, Mother and I. Outright. We had to move anyway, our terrace
house was all steps, it even had steps up to the front door. Hopeless
with this thing. That's the main disadvantage, it won't go up stairs.
Only thing we didn't like out here was the noise of the aircraft -- we
didn't know we were so near the airport when we bought the place.
Nowhere is perfect. Like the smog in Los Angeles. Is it as bad as
they say?

Emma Only if you like to see the tops of the buildings. But we
can get to the coast from where we live in twenty minutes.

*Kate lifts herself up by her hands again. Emma places her hands on
Kate's knees in sympathy*

Is it bad?

Kate I've adjusted to it now. Everybody tried to comfort me at first
by saying how lucky I was to be alive at all. I have to keep asking

myself is it better to live like this, or would it have been better to
have gone with Daddy. I suppose it's better to be alive. Amazing
what you can get used to if you have to.

Emma No hope at all then?

Kate About walking? No. None.

Emma What about ...?

Kate Sex? I've adjusted to that too. Like nuns must do, I expect.
Some paraplegics marry of course, to other paraplegics usually -
- have babies even. I'm not saying it isn't a problem, but I think I've
come to terms with it.

Panda There you go, you great nit, deluding yourself again.

Emma What happened to — I've forgotten his name — that chap
doing history that was so keen on you? When I left it looked as if
you and he ...

Kate He's at some university up north, lecturing. I hear him on the
radio occasionally. He's got a wife and daughter.

Emma Kate ... are you *really* happy?

Kate Of course I am. You don't expect me to sit and mope, do you?
That's not me, you should know that.

Emma But that's why I couldn't figure out why you stopped
writing.

Kate I've *told* you ...

Emma Kate, you don't make many friends in a lifetime, you know.
Real friends. You have to keep in touch with them, or the bonds
wither — and there's nothing left.

Kate I'm well aware of that. (*She fills the glasses*) Now! I want to
hear all about Hollywood. Do you get to see the film stars?

Emma Everybody asks the same question.

Kate Well, do you?

Emma (*deliberately blasé*) You get used to it.

Kate (*excited*) Who've you seen? Do you talk to them? Where do
you see them?

Emma Oh, in the restaurants, in the street, in the supermarkets.
They're only human beings, you know, like· you and me. I mean,
they *live* there, don't they?

Kate Of course, they're your neighbours! Oh I'm so jealous, Emma.
Do you go to parties, wild parties, things like that?

Emma Yes, Larry and I go to parties. They're not all that wild. TV people mainly, actors from the soap operas.

Kate Who? Who?

Emma I wouldn't know where to start. You probably don't get their shows over here anyway.

Kate You don't know how lucky you are!

Emma (*deliberately too blasé*) The novelty wears off.

Kate Strange isn't it? You were always the quiet one – the timid one – do you remember?

Emma And you were the glamour puss, the good time girl.

Kate And now I go to bed every night just as you're getting dolled up to go out, I expect. Oh, I'm so happy for you, Emma – and so jealous! Here ... (*She starts to fill Emma's glass*)

Emma No, no more, Kate. I've got to drive back. Look, I'll tell you what, I'll go back home now and you get an early night. I'll come back as soon as I can tomorrow and stay till it's time for my plane.

Kate No, don't go, Emma. We can talk, all night if you wish.

Emma I've got to pack my bits and pieces anyway, and say goodbye to my folks. I only really drove out to see if I could find you. I'll see you tomorrow. Early.

Emma All right, Emma. Come as soon as you can.

Emma Yes I will. (*She kisses Kate, starts to go, then sees the easel and looks at the painting*) Who paints? You?

Kate Yes ... it's a sort of therapy ... they tell me.

Emma It's terrific!

Panda Bloody liar.

Kate Do you really think so?

Emma It's great! And you were hopeless at art in school. (*She goes to the other canvases and looks at them*) Are these yours too?

Kate Yes.

Emma (*a shade over enthusiastic*) They're – smashing!

Panda They all go through the same performance! She doesn't mean it, you know, she's just trying to be kind.

Emma Oh I like this one! Is it a view from the window?

Kate Er -- no ... It's just an imaginary landscape.

Panda Why the hell don't you tell her – you copied it from a

picture postcard!
Emma I must fly. Bye Kate.

Emma goes

Kate wheels herself back to the bed and gets in

Kate I thought you were horrid tonight, Panda. Horrid!
Panda Oh go to sleep! (*Sarcastically*) Happy little Kate! You've "adjusted" to everything, haven't you? *You* don't mind not be able to walk, do you? *You* don't mind not being able to have a feller, do you? Oh no! You make me sick!
Kate That's enough, Panda!
Panda *You* don't mind spending the rest of your life doing nothing more exciting than nursing the sores on your bottom, do you?
Kate Good-*night*, Panda! (*She turns off the light*)

The night light fades to Black-out

Kate exits

Gradually morning light appears behind the curtains. Kate is not in bed and the wheelchair has gone

Mrs Ponsello lets herself in, looks in at the bed, then looks into the kitchen

Mrs Ponsello You're up early. What's up? Couldn't sleep?
Kate (*off*) Big day! I'm expecting someone. Someone special.
Mrs Ponsello Oh yes? What y' doin'? Bakin?
Kate Ginger cake. It's in the oven. I'm just clearing up. My visitor loves ginger cake. Always did.
Mrs Ponsello Here, let me do that —
Kate (*off*) No! I've just about finished.
Mrs Ponsello I'll straighten the bed then. (*She takes off her coat, opens the curtains, and starts making the bed*)

Kate wheels herself in. She is dressed and wearing a pretty apron

So who's this special someone then?

Kate You'll never guess. My oldest friend.

Mrs Ponsello Can't be all that good a friend, can he? 'Aven't seen much of 'im whilst I've bin with you, 'ave we?

Kate It's not a he, it's a she, and she hasn't been because she lives in Los Angeles.

Mrs Ponsello American, is she?

Kate No, she met this boy Larry. He came over to our university for a term from the USC — that's the University of Southern California -- on an exchange, and he swept her off her feet, whipped her off home, married her and I've not seen her since.

Mrs Ponsello Was that before ...? (*meaning the accident*)

Kate I was going to be her bridesmaid — the only person there from England. Had my ticket booked.

Mrs Ponsello What about her folks?

Kate They wouldn't go — her father won't fly and her mother is a rotten sailor.

Mrs Ponsello Silly buggers!

Kate They were dead against her marrying him anyway. They didn't like him and they didn't want her to go. Then this happened and I didn't get there either.

Mrs Ponsello What a shame! And she's coming today? 'Ave y' had a letter?

Kate She was here last night after you left. (*With a strange look*) Do you know, when I woke up this morning I was sure I'd dreamt it. I wondered whether she had really been here. I sat up in bed and I thought — was it a dream? Have I just dreamt it? Then I saw that.

Mrs Ponsello What?

Kate That bottle of gin. We drank it — neat! It was marvellous! I hate gin.

Mrs Ponsello So do I. But I drink it as well.

They laugh together

Kate We'd have finished the bottle, only she had to drive back.

Mrs Ponsello What's 'er name?

Kate Emma. She's flying back today, I'm afraid.

Mrs Ponsello I'm sorry I promised to go to Mrs Coombs now.

The bell rings

Kate That might be her!

Mrs Ponsello goes out to answer the door. Emma comes in and hugs Kate. Mrs Ponsello follows her in

Emma, this is Mrs Ponsello, my absolute treasure. I don't know what I'd have done without her.

Emma Hi, treasure.

Mrs Ponsello I've just bin 'earin' about you, 'ow you two were friends.

Emma (*with her arm round Kate*) Most wonderful girl in the world, Kate. You'll have found that out, won't you? Pity I live so far away.

Kate Didn't seem to bother you when Larry arrived on the scene. You waltzed off as if there was no-one else in the world.

Emma You'd have done the same, then, wouldn't you? Admit it.

Mrs Ponsello Love's young dream!

Kate It didn't happen to me, did it, so we'll never know.

Emma I honestly thought I was just going for a few weeks, to meet his folks. Well, you know, don't you? Never occurred to me that I wouldn't get back. Mother had to pack up all my things and send them over. I suddenly found myself caught up in a completely new world, England seemed a million miles away.

Mrs Ponsello Didn't y' get to feelin' homesick ever?

Emma Oh no. It was too exciting.

Mrs Ponsello My old man's Italian an' 'e's bin homesick ever since I've known 'im. Nothin' 'ere is as good as Italy accordin' to 'im; the food, the clothes, the music, specially the weather. Anyway, 'e's gettin' 'is wish and' goin' back. *I'll* be 'omesick, I know I will. I am already an' we 'aven't gone yet.

Kate You could always come back.

Mrs Ponsello You don't know 'im, 'e'll never come back, 'e's pig-

'eaded. When they made 'im redundant 'e got very bitter an' I don't blame 'im. They didn't 'ave a harder worker in that firm. 'E was flabbergasted when they told 'im. Anyroad, I've no time to stand chattin'. Is there anythin' I can fetch on my way back?

Kate Yes please. I've written a list out. (*She hands her a piece of paper*) Any time will do.

Mrs Ponsello 'Ope y' 'ave a pleasant journey back.

Emma Thanks. Have a happy day.

Mrs Ponsello (*surprised at this remark*) Oh! Thanks!

Mrs Ponsello goes

Emma I take it you've got someone else fixed up to replace her.

Kate (*taking off her apron*) Of course I have.

Panda Liar!

Emma I'm glad about that. I suppose there are always people ready to help ...

Kate ... anyone in my condition? Yes, they fall over themselves, oozing with sympathy. You don't have to worry about me, really Emma. *I* don't worry about it.

Panda Huh!

Emma Kate darling! I want you to promise me that you'll keep in touch regularly from now on.

Kate I'll ... send you a card ... on your birthday.

Emma You ... pig!

Kate There are a million questions I want to ask you that I've thought of since last night.

Emma Such as?

Kate Well — your wedding. Have you got any pictures?

Emma Not with me. Mother has some.

Kate Did you — have a bridesmaid? Instead of me?

Emma A cousin of Larry's. Sweet girl, Greta her name is. I'd only met her the week before the wedding -- it wasn't like having you there. Do you know, her parents actually named her after Greta Garbo because they liked her in the movies!

Kate (*like a teenager*) I — er — don't suppose you've seen Greta Garbo in Hollywood ...?

Emma Oh for heaven's sake grow up, Kate.

Kate (*like a bobby-soxer*) Did you ever see Cary Grant?

Emma He was your favourite, wasn't he?

Kate Still is. I saw him on the telly a while back and I nearly swooned all over again.

Emma Well, I saw him in a restaurant once, sitting in a corner with a girl half his age.

Kate Oh you lucky devil! You *saw* him! Is he as handsome as —?

Emma Just the same as on the screen. What can I smell?

Kate That's the ginger cake I'm baking. Specially for you.

Emma Terrrific!

Kate Now tell me about the baby. Have you thought of names yet?

Emma Give us a chance!

Kate Have you got nice neighbours? I want to know everything. I think that's very important, neighbours. My nearest is Mr Cartwright in that bungalow with the slate roof up the hill -- but he's an odd one, that chap, not at all friendly. I don't think we've exchanged a dozen words since I've lived here. There are some nice people in the village though. They send me marmalade and lemon curd and apple pies, things like that, with Mrs Ponsello. They don't call to see me very often.

Panda You don't make them all that welcome when they do come, do you?

Emma Oh, my neighbours are OK I guess. But it's on the surface mainly. There's something odd behind all the smiles and the sentimentality, something I never noticed over here. A sort of hardness ... ruthlessness. That vicious streak that runs through American films and the TV programmes -- you find it in the home as well ... and in marriage ...

Kate I don't —

Emma They can be very unkind to each other. That's what *I* find, anyway. Outwardly they're all sunshine and sweetness, and fun, but they can be cruel, self-centred, unthinking ... they can hurt you terribly. (*Suddenly she breaks down and falls to her knees, her head in Kate's lap*)

Kate Emma! Darling! What's the matter?

Emma I don't want to go back, Kate. I don't want to go back!

Kate Emma! What is it?
Emma It's ... awful ... (*She sobs bitterly*)
Kate Emma darling!
Emma I really came to tell my parents – I can't take any more! But it's the same as it was before. I can't talk to them. I couldn't tell them...
Kate Tell them what?

Emma calms down a little

Emma I'm sorry, Kate. You've got troubles of your own. Mine are nothing compared to yours.
Kate Is it the baby?
Emma No. Yes.
Kate What do you mean, no, yes?
Emma Look – forget it. I didn't intend to —
Kate What is it? You can tell me. You can tell Kate. We always told each other everything.
Emma Well ... to start with, the baby isn't Larry's. (*She breaks down again*)

Kate looks at her for a moment, speechless, waiting for her to continue

   I came to talk to my parents about it. I had to talk to someone. I wanted to ask their advice – but they're so stupid! I've been here three weeks and I still haven't been able to tell them.
Kate Does Larry know it's not his baby?
Emma He doesn't even know I'm pregnant.

A pause

Kate Can't you ... you know ...? You're not very far gone, are you? You could ... I mean ... can't you tell him it's his?
Emma Larry and I haven't been living together for a year. He left me. No, that's not true – I threw him out.
Kate You threw him out!

Emma Kate— it was awful! Take my advice, don't get married! He was supposed to be going off on these assignments, filming trips, but some of the times he was carrying on with this — this long thin blonde streak who works in the cutting-room. I got a phone call one night from a man — wouldn't tell me his name, but he knew what was going on well enough. He seemed to get a stack of pleasure out of telling me, too. I didn't believe him at first. So I began checking up. It was true all right. Too true. One night I actually saw them go into a motel together! I stood outside, watching ... a long time, till they turned out the light. I meant to go in and surprise them at it, to humiliate them, but I funked it. I went home and cried my eyes out. When Larry came back the next evening I asked him where he'd been, sort of casually, and he gave me a detailed description of the filming he'd done, a hundred miles away from that motel, and how tough it had been. (*Crying again*) The lying bastard! We had one helluva row! At least *I* did, I really blew my top. What annoyed me as much as anything was his complacency, as if it was ... nothing! Larry actually had the idea that I wouldn't *mind* him having the odd mistress now and again. He said all his friends did. Can you imagine? Can you imagine how I felt? The following night, when he came home, he found all his clothes strewn over the garden and I'd bolted the doors. I didn't let him in.

Kate Oh, Emma!

Emma He knocked and banged, then, in the end, he went away.

Kate And was that *it*?

Emma He phoned several times afterwards but I hung up on him as soon as I heard his voice. And I kept the doors bolted. Do you know, Kate, it's amazing how quickly love can turn to hate. In a second!

Kate smoothes Emma's hair in sympathy

Then he moved in with her, into a crummy little apartment, and stopped phoning. And that was that! It got so I kept sitting by the phone hoping he would ring, just to have the pleasure of hanging up on him again! I can't tell you how unhappy I was, Kate.

Kate My poor Emma.

Emma There was no-one to talk to. No-one! I gave up my job. I began to live like a hermit. The only time I went out was when I ran out of food.

Kate What about all your friends – all those television people and stars you used to meet?

Emma Stars? I never met any stars. I never *saw* any. The only people I ever met were folks like you and me who work for a living doing ordinary jobs, go out once a fortnight if they're lucky. Hollywood! It's an obscenity! There's a lot to be said for dear old sensible England, you know, Kate.

Kate So how do you come to be pregnant?

Emma Well, one of the neighbours began to show more than an interest in me. He became a sort of … father confessor – the only person I could talk to. Very nice guy, originally from Texas, and getting on a bit. Bit of a joker really – used to play small parts in cowboy movies one time, but he works in an office now. We always got on well, even before Larry went.

Kate So it's his child?

Emma (*after a quick pause*) Yes.

Kate Does he know?

Emma Yes.

Kate And what does he say, this cowboy?

Emma Say? What can he say? He's married. He's got a family.

Kate Good God!

Emma Do you know why I came? It wasn't really to talk to my folks, I knew that wouldn't work. I was just running away. I couldn't stand it any more. But that's no good either. I'll have to face the music here too. You can't run away from your troubles.

Kate But you must have told your parents you're pregnant.

Emma They think the child is Larry's. They just assumed. They don't know we've split up. What should I do, Kate?

Kate What does your cowboy friend suggest?

Emma He wants me to have an abortion. Get rid of it.

Kate (*quickly*) No! No, Emma! (*A pause*) Listen, don't go back! Stay here. With me. To hell with them all! *We'll* bring up your baby, it will be *ours*.

Emma Stay here?

Kate There's a lovely bedroom upstairs. It was Mother's. You could move in today. Right now. Mrs Ponsello has always kept the room ready in case of a visitor, not that I've ever had one. I've enough money for our keep, we wouldn't need to worry about that. We wouldn't need to worry about a thing. Oh, do stay, Emma. It's lovely here in the summertime, wait till you see it.

Emma Roses round the door and all that?

Kate No, but there's honeysuckle. It's a real picture, honest! And no-one would bother us.

Emma (*warming to the idea*) I could look after you, couldn't I?

Kate And I could care for the baby. Oh, Emma, yes.

Emma I could get a divorce, I suppose ... and to hell with Larry ...

Kate *And* your cowboy.

Emma Kate, do you think I could? Do you think it's possible.

Kate Of course it is. It would be *our* baby. I'd love that. *Our baby.* Yours and mine. What's to stop us?

Emma (*hugging her*) Kate! I do love you! I feel better already. Here I am, all wrapped up in my own little worries and – and ... you were always good for me. You've actually managed to cheer me up! For the first time since I've been home. I've been crying myself to sleep every night, worrying about my problems.

Kate There are no problems – they're all solved. You'll have your baby here. We'll be a two-parent family, you and me. Perfect parents!

Emma How do you do it? How do you keep so – sunny? What's your secret?

Kate There is no secret. I believe in happiness, that's all. That's what living is all about. Happiness is the objective of everything; religion, psychology, politics, medicine, they're all simply in pursuit of happiness.

Emma But how can you be happy when the whole world starts to fall in?

Kate All right then, *be* miserable – if that's what makes you happy.

Gradually, looking into each other's eyes, they smile. Then they start to laugh. The laughter becomes almost hysterical. They are like young schoolgirls again. The phone rings. Kate, still laughing, answers it

Yes?... Who?... (*Surprised*) Oh, hello!... I'm fine, thanks..... Yes, I'm much better.... Just a tick. (*To Emma*) It's your mother.

Emma (*taking the phone*) Yes, Mother. ... Did they give you the number? ... One sec. (*To Kate*) Got a pencil?

Kate There's one there, on the table.

Emma (*taking down the number*) Yes... yes... I'll ring them now. Thanks, Mother. (*She hangs up*) The airline wants me to ring right away about something. Do you mind?

Kate No, of course not.

Emma dials

How did your mother know my number?

Emma (*waiting for her call to connect*) I gave it to her. (*Into the phone*) Oh hello, Mrs Emma Lynn here. I understand you want to speak to me about Los Angeles Flight LA four-nine-seven. ... Thanks. (*To Kate*) I thought Mother might get in touch with you after I left. You don't mind, do you? (*Into the phone*) Oh hello. ... Yes. ... (*Her expression changes*) When? ... Just a minute. (*To Kate, covering the phone*) The plane I was supposed to go on has had to land in New York with engine trouble. They are offering me a seat on an earlier flight if I can get there straightaway.

Kate Well tell them — you're not going!

Pause. Emma thinks, and looks at her watch

What are you waiting for? Tell them!

Emma I'm trying to think! (*Into the phone*) Can I call you back? ... Oh! ... (*She bites her lip and looks at Kate. After a pause*) All right, I'll be there. Thanks. (*She hangs up*) They had to know immediately — there's a waiting list.

Kate looks at her aggressively. Emma's face takes on a sympathetic, apologetic look

It was a marvellous offer, Kate ...

Kate Was? It's the perfect solution — to everything.

Emma No. It's the kind of solution Hollywood likes, that's all.

Kate What's wrong with it? It'll be great – for both of us. For all three of us. Call them back.

Emma You make it sound so simple.

Kate You've only got one life, Emma. *One*. And this is it. Don't ruin it! Don't throw away this chance, Emma.

Emma I have to go back.

Kate But why? It's crazy!

Emma There's a house out there, full of my things. I've still got a husband out there you know, even though ... And there's the father of my child, I don't see why he should get away scot free.

Kate To hell with your things! There's everything we can possibly need here. Let Larry keep your things. What are you worrying about things for?

Emma Kate, let's face reality, both of us. I can't just —

Kate Yes you can!

They face each other

        Please stay, Emma. (*Imploringly*) It'll work out fine, you'll see. You'll never regret it. (*Getting almost hysterical*) Emma – please stay, please ...

Panda Go on, beg! Make a fool of yourself!

Emma It was wishful thinking, I'm afraid. We shouldn't have let ourselves get carried away like that.

Kate No, it wasn't. There needs to be purpose in life. There needs to be someone that cares for you, somebody that loves you, somebody that's prepared to accept you as you are. You'd find that here, Emma, I promise you. And so would I.

They look at each other for a moment; Kate pleadingly, Emma undecidedly

Emma I'd – better start if I'm going to get that plane. I have to hand the car back yet. (*Coming to her*) Goodbye, Kate. I'm sorry I couldn't spend more time with you.

Kate (*backing away in her chair*) You fool! (*In an outburst of* *temper*) You great simpleton! I offer you a way out of all your troubles and you can't even see it! You're just too damned obstinate to see it!

Emma Kate, please try to understand ...

Kate You always were a stupid ninny, weren't you? Ever since I've known you. Why in hell should I expect you to change!

Emma Kate!

Kate We all warned you about Larry, didn't we, but would you take any notice? Oh no, not you! You wouldn't even listen! You weren't the only one he was fooling around with, you know.

Emma Oh I knew you all fancied him. I knew that. Of course I did. But I was the one he wanted to marry, wasn't I?

Kate That was only a ploy, you fool – to get you laid. You weren't the only one he dangled a wedding ring in front of.

Emma That's not true!

Kate I'm afraid it is.

Panda What the hell are you doing? Stop it, for God's sake!

Emma Who else did he ask? Who else?

Kate Several.

Emma Who?

Kate Me for one, if you must know!

Panda You pig! You bloody *pig*!

Emma I don't believe it.

Kate Go ahead, believe what you want.

Panda Emma's supposed to be your friend! What are you trying to do?

Emma He actually asked you to marry him?

Kate I've told you all I'm going to.

Emma And did you sleep with him?

Kate I'm telling you no more!

Emma Did you? Kate, *did you*?

Kate (*hysterically*) Yes! Yes, yes! So did Chrissie Blyth – and Maureen. And that little bitch with the gold teeth!

Emma I don't believe you.

Kate Believe what you want! He didn't expect you to go to America with him, you know. He might have asked you, but he didn't expect you to go. He asked everyone. You were just too dumb to know what was going on.

Emma That's not true!

Kate Oh no? Ring up Chrissie Blyth, go on. Ask her!

Panda Have you gone off your rocker?

Emma Why are you telling me this now? Do you think it will make me feel better?

Kate I don't care how you feel. You're a fool. You always were and you always will be! Why should I care about fools!

Emma And you're so clever, aren't you? What was it you said - - you have one life and this is it! Well you're making the most of living yours, aren't you, locking yourself away here miles from anywhere and everyone and keeping your whereabouts a secret. You're like a damned prisoner sentenced to solitary, only you've done the sentencing yourself. Fine life that is! It's not a life at all, it's an existence, sitting waiting until you snuff it. You're facing up to nothing. Nothing! I might have made a mess of my life, but at least I'm prepared to face up to it!

Kate I'm sorry you came! What the hell did you have to come for!

Emma Yes, well perhaps I'd better go. Sorry it hasn't worked out. (*She goes to the door and stops*) Goodbye, Kate. I'll write to you.

Kate Don't bother! (*She swings her chair round, her back to Emma*)

Emma stands looking at her for a moment

Panda You idiot! You *idiot*!

  Emma hesitates, then goes

Kate cries. There is the sound of the car driving off. Kate eases herself in the chair as if in pain

  Your cake's ready. I can smell burning.

Kate Let the bloody thing burn! I don't care if the whole house burns down. With you and me in it! (*She cries*)

Panda Who's the stupid ninny now? You really believed that silly little pipe-dream, didn't you? You and Emma living together, bringing up a kid! You'd have loved that, wouldn't you, mothering the two of them!

Kate (*shrieking*) Oh shut up!

Panda And what would you do when some man came along and fancied Emma, eh? She's not a bad-looking dish, Emma isn't.

Kate (*with her hands over her ears*) Shut up, will you! Shut up!

Panda The fellers always preferred *you* to Emma, but not anymore. You'd look a fine sight, wouldn't you, when she suddenly upped and went, and took the kid with her, just when you thought everything was settled.

Kate Shut up! Shut up!

Panda What's the use of kidding yourself all the time? You're on your own now, girl! Nobody's going to come and live here. Get used to the idea. It's you and me and that box of paints. And you're no painter either, get used to *that* idea too. You keep trying to conjure up some little Disney world of your own. You *visit* Disneyland for a day, you know, you don't bloody well *live* in it.

Kate wheels herself to the bed and throws Panda across the room in temper and with such force that she falls forward out of the chair and on to the floor. She collapses in tears. A plane goes over, low. Kate looks up and listens

Kate If only I could get on one of those things and fly away ... (*She drags herself over to the bedside table, takes a handkerchief from the drawer, and wipes her eyes. Suddenly she stops crying, listens, but does not look round*)

There is a strange change of lighting as if the sun had appeared and thrown a ray of light into the room through a haze

   Quietly, Emma appears at the back, a suitcase in hand

Kate stops crying, as if she senses the presence of Emma

   (*Quietly, without looking round*) Emma?

Emma drops the suitcase and comes over to her. Kate throws her arms around Emma's knees and hugs her, laughing and crying with joy. Emma smiles

C<small>URTAIN</small>

NB. Ideally, it should be left uncertain whether Emma really has returned, or whether this too is merely self-deception on Kate's part motivated by wishful thinking

FURNITURE AND PROPERTY LIST

On stage: Bed. *On it:* bedclothes, large Panda (with movable mouth)
                Bedside table. *On it:* lamp, telephone. *In drawer:* handkerchief
                Chair. *On it:* **Kate**'s nightclothes and dressing-gown
                Small table. *On it:* newspapers, books, painting items
                Armchair
                Mrs Ponsello's coat
                Easel. *On it:* canvas
                Various canvases leaning against the wall
                Curtains drawn

Off stage: 2 glasses, bottle of gin (**Kate**)

DURING BLACK-OUT ON PAGE 18

Strike: Wheelchair
                Kate's clothes

Off stage: Suitcase (**Emma**)

Personal: **Kate:** wheelchair with cushion
                Emma: wristwatch

LIGHTING PLOT

Practical fittings required: table lamps

Interior. The same scene throughout

To open: Practicals on with covering spots

Cue 1	**Kate** turns out the light	Page 7)
	Snap off practicals and covering spots leaving dim night light	

Cue 2	**Kate** turns on the light	(Page 7)
	Snap on practicals and covering spots	

Cue 3	**Kate** turns off the light	(Page 18)
	Snap off practicals and covering spots, fade to black-out	

Cue 4	When ready	(Page 18)
	Gradually bring up morning light through curtains	

Cue 5	**Mrs Ponsello** opens the curtains	(Page 18)
	Increase daylight effect	

Cue 6	**Kate** suddenly stops crying and listens	(Page 31)
	Bring up hazy sun-ray effect	

EFFECTS PLOT

Cue 1   When ready   (Page 1)
         Phone

Cue 2   **Mrs Ponsello**: "...she's slow at these things."   (Page 1)
         Plane goes over

Cue 3   **Mrs Ponsello** goes   (Page 4)
         Plane goes over

Cue 4   **Kate** snuggles in   (Page 7)
         *Plane goes over. Pause, doorbell. Pause, doorbell
            again*

Cue 5   **Kate** (*off*): "There!"   (Page 8)
         Front door opens and closes

Cue 6   **Mrs Ponsello** lets herself in   (Page 18)
         Front door opens and closes

Cue 7   **Mrs Ponsello**: "...go to Mrs Coombs now."   (Page 20)
         Doorbell

Cue 8   **Mrs Ponsello** goes out to answer the door   (Page 20)
         Front door opens and closes

Cue 9   **Kate and Emma** laugh   (Page 26)
         Phone

Cue 10 **Emma** hesitates, then goes   (Page 30)
          Front door opens and closes, pause, car driving off

Cue 11 **Kate** collapses in tears   (Page 31)
          Plane goes over low